THE ONE HOUR PURIM PRIMER

"This book represents another eminently readable, wonderfully practical and strikingly lucid approach to transmitting ideas and celebrating a major Jewish calendar event."

Rabbi Michel and Rebbitzen Feige Twerski –Milwaukee
Congregation Beth Jehudah

The One Hour Purim Primer
by
Shimon Apisdorf

published by

66 North Merkle Road Columbus, Ohio 43209
(614) 338-0774
New Address, August 1995
2505 Summerson Road Baltimore, Maryland 21209
1-800-LEVIATHAN

ISBN 1-881927-04-0

PRINTED IN THE UNITED STATES OF AMERICA

Group Sales: The One Hour Purim Primer, Passover Survival Kit, Survival Kit Haggadah, and Rosh Hashanah Yom Kippur Survival Kit are available to schools, synagogues and community organizations by special order. See inside back cover.

ACKNOWLEDGEMENTS

Donna Cohen, Josh Greenberg, Rabbi Jonathan Rosenberg, Motti, Dima, Eugene, Minga, Rada, April, Svieta, Julia, Julianna, Victor, Daniel, David, Cyd, Martin, Valery, Dennis, Naomi, Sophia, Fira, Abraham, Boris, Reuven and Jenny, Albert and the van, Terry Sankey and Select Design, Bonnie, Lori and Executive Office Place, Rick Cohen, Rabbi Pinchas Winston, Rabbi Aryeh Kaltman, Uncle Harry, Mike Berenstein, Michael Hart, William Schottenstein, Jake Koval, Joe and Helen Berman, Blair Axel, Dov Friedberg, Sharon Goldinger and PeopleSpeak, Rabbi Elbaz, Rabbi Millen, CTA, Rabbi Asher Resnick, Ben Rothke, Jodie Zuckerman, and Our Faithful Pink Example Sheet.

APPRECIATION

Sherri Cohen, dedicated typist. Amy "say little and do much" Greenberg. Congregation Ahavas Sholom, a spiritual home; a sanctuary of kedusha. Ann Apisdorf, a wonderful aunt, friend, sister, sister-in-law and teammate. Russell Simmons, thanks for teaching me how to fish. Rabbi Noah Weinberg, Rosh Hayeshiva and source of inspiration.

SPECIAL THANKS

Mr. and Mrs. David and Bernice Apisdorf. Though you let go of our hands, you never leave our sides. Thanks for the love, the laughs and the encouragement.

Mr. and Mrs. Robert and Charlotte Rothenburg. If all hearts were as kind as yours, no hearts would ever be broken.

Esther Rivka, Ditzah Leah, Yitzchak Ben Zion. May your souls always radiate with the joyous light you bring into this world.

Miriam. Your presence makes my grapefruit meaningful. Each day with you brings new lessons; in love, growth and gratitude.

Hakadosh Baruch Hu, source of all blessings.

CONTENTS

1

INTRODUCTION

Science, Cyberspace and the Soul

Something is going on out there. One need not be an astute social analyst to see that the search for a metaphysic that speaks to our time no longer emanates from the fringe, nor is it the sole domain of those who seek to live life in a New Age sort of way. While science and technology are changing our world more rapidly than we can keep up with, the timeless questions of existence and the human condition are sounding an ever more resonant chord.

The fields of science and technology are inherently progressive. Breakthroughs and advances are the products of new knowledge based on more experimentation, tests and evidence than anything that preceded them. In the technological realm, what's newer is generally what's better. At the same time, people are seriously questioning whether all these developments necessarily bring in their wake better ways of understanding and dealing with life. There is a growing realization that those of an earlier time, those who could never have conceived of the internet or a modem, could, and did, devote a great deal of thought to matters of human fulfillment, the meaning of life and issues of identity. Today, from the boardroom to the ballpark, matters of the soul, of a mind-body relationship, of values and of a spiritual dimension to living have entered the mainstream of social consciousness and discussion.

The National Institute of Health, a bastion of biological reductionism which has long viewed human beings as just another dish of chemical reactions, has allocated two million dollars to establish a Panel of Mind-Body Interventions. Harvard Medical School now holds seminars examining the frontiers of mind-body medicine. For a sense of the public pulse, one need look no further than the *New York Times'* bestseller list where over twenty-five percent of the titles in recent years have been books related to spirituality. *The Road Less Traveled,* a book about spiritual growth, has been a bestseller for over five hundred weeks. And Phil Jackson, a six-foot, ten-inch, ex-New York Knick and Buddhist, successfully coached Michael Jordan and the Chicago Bulls to three NBA championships while employing zen techniques with his players. Clearly, something is going on out there.

The Millenium Shift

The year 2000 is closing in all around us. As history moves closer to this mythical watershed, people of every ilk are looking not only backwards and forwards, but more importantly, inwards. More and more the coming calendar shift is catching people's cosmic attention. "Where are we headed?" they ask. "Where should we be headed? What does it all mean? Is there an ultimate purpose or meaning to my life, or have I just been set hopelessly adrift?" Simply put, people want to know, "What's it all about?" And this time the *it* is not outer space, but inner space. *It* is life.

The Jewish calendar takes a much broader view of human history than does our civil calendar. If you look at a Jewish calendar, you will find that we are in the year 5755, not 1995. Thus, the Jewish calendar has no millennium shift for another two hundred and forty-five years. Nonetheless, Judaism would always applaud any efforts at introspection, any attempts to grapple with life's ultimate questions and every aspiration to uncover a deeper dimension to living.

Look Again: At Purim and Life

A steady theme throughout the story and holiday of Purim is the idea of seeing beneath the surface. The Book of Esther tells the Purim story and is the only book in the Bible which never mentions the name of G-d; yet at every turn in the story one can't help but sense a transcendent presence. Purim is the only holiday in which we are told not only to eat and drink, but to actually get drunk! (See page 30 for a discussion of this issue.) Yet, while the observance of the holiday includes eating, drinking, costumes and parties, both the great Kabbalist, Rabbi Isaac Luria and Maimonides, the renowned sage and philosopher, assure us that Purim is a day whose spirituality is rivaled by no other. And the Hebrew term for the Book of Esther, *Megillat Esther,* when literally translated, means to reveal (*megillat*) that which is hidden (*esther*). From all sides the holiday of Purim calls out to us, in fact challenges us, to look beyond the surface.

The wonders of the world around us are without end. Majesty and awe are commonplace in nature, but there is more to this awe than meets the eye. The complexities of the human organism are just beginning to be understood. Yet, this Homo sapien is not just another genus or species. There is far more to the human being than meets the microscope. In all aspects of life, Judaism looks at one level and then proceeds to perceive and reveal quite another. In every detail of living, Judaism sees a dimension of an ever-deeper life form, and a richer quality of potential. It is to these depths of perception and living that Purim calls us.

I recently had a conversation with an accomplished graphic designer from California named Heidi. Quite to my surprise she told me that, "I was born Jewish. I've never really done much Jewish stuff, but lately I've been wondering if there could be any spirituality in Judaism. You know," she continued, "you can begin a conversation for one reason and find out that it was supposed to lead you in a direction you never imagined."

"Heidi," I wrote in the copy of a book I sent her, "sometimes the things we are looking for are hidden in places we would least expect to find them." Like Purim. Often referred to as a "minor festival," Purim is in fact a major source of wisdom and spiritual inspiration.

The One Hour Purim Primer has been written for everyone who never dreamed that there could be more to Judaism than what they encountered in the world of suburban Jewry. Indeed, just as there is far more to Purim than meets the eye, so there is far more to Judaism than most of us were led to believe. This book is an attempt to cast a ray of light into the subterranean domain of Jewish wisdom and spirituality. Far from inaccessible or foreboding, once we venture beneath the surface of Judaism, we will find an enlightening and enchanting inner world — a world of experience and thought that speaks to us in the context of our lives today while simultaneously lifting our vision of what we — and the world — can be tomorrow.

2

THE BLUR OF HISTORY

When we think of the ancient world we think of civilizations like the Egyptians, Persians, Babylonians, Greeks and Romans. We think of cities like Antioch, Alexandria, Babylon and Rome; of rivers like the Nile, the Tigris and the Euphrates; and of rulers like Ramses, Hammurabi, Xerxes and Alexander. The truth be known, for many of us this jumble of names is a historical stew of people and places which has little, if any, meaning. At the same time, for Jews of another epoch — Jews who were Jews just like we are — these names and places were as real to them as Warsaw, Berlin and Stalin were to our great-grandparents, and as alive as Chicago, Miami and Saddam Hussein are to us.

The story of Purim is set in an era which saw the Jewish people sovereign in the land of Israel. That same period was witness to the end of their sovereignty and the destruction of the First Temple at the hands of Nebuchadnezzar and the Babylonians. And the immediate events which surround Purim are the defeat of those same Babylonians at the hands of the ascendant power from Media and Persia. The defeat of the Babylonians brought the Jews under the rule of Darius the Mede, Cyrus the Persian and eventually Achashverosh, ruler of the vast Persian Empire and co-star of the Book of Esther.

A Thousand Years in Three Pages

(Or Your Money Back)

The following chronology, followed by a brief historical overview, will provide a working knowledge of the major events which precede and surround the story of Purim. Far from exhaustive, this section is meant only to provide general historical context in the place of general historical fuzziness.

OVERVIEW
Jewish History

Abraham and Sarah	2080 / 1671 BCE
Egyptian slavery begins	2332 / 1428 BCE
Exodus and Torah at Mt. Sinai	2448 / 1312 BCE
Jewish People enter Israel	2488 / 1272 BCE
First Temple built	2935 / 825 BCE
First Temple destroyed; Babylonian exile begins	3338 / 422 BCE
Purim events	3405 / 355 BCE
Second Temple built	3408 / 352 BCE
Miracle of Chanukah	3622 / 139 BCE
Second Temple destroyed; Roman exile begins	3830 / 70 CE
Babylonian Talmud compiled	4260 / 500 CE
First Crusade	4856 / 1096 CE
Expulsion of French Jewry	5155 / 1475 CE
Spread of Chassidism	5532 / 1772 CE
First Zionist Congress	5657 / 1897 CE
Rebirth of Israel	5708 / 1948 CE
Persian Gulf War	5751 / 1991 CE

OVERVIEW
Purim Period

10,000 scholars and leaders exiled to Babylonia	3327 / 434 BCE
Nebuchadnezzar and Babylonians destroy Temple and exile Jews	3338 / 372 BCE
Media and Persia join forces to conquer Babylonia	3388 / 372 BCE
Cyrus becomes king of Persian empire	3390 / 371 BCE
Achashverosh ascends throne of Persian empire	3401 / 360 BCE
Haman becomes prime minister of Persia; Esther becomes the queen	3404 / 356 BCE
The miracle and victory of Purim occur; Mordecai is the new prime minister of Persia	3405 / 355 BCE
Saddam Hussein declares himself to be the "new Nebuchadnezzar", attacks Israel, and is defeated in the Gulf War which ends on Purim	5751 / 1991 CE

Making a Little Sense of History

The Jewish people, led by Joshua, entered the land of Israel in the year 1272 BCE. After settling and developing the land and establishing both a monarchy and a sophisticated legal and judicial system, the building of the First Temple was begun in the year 832 BCE by King David and completed in the year 825 BCE by his son, King Solomon. The First Temple stood for 410 years. During that time a vibrant Jewish community flourished in the land of Israel with Jerusalem and the Temple as its spiritual, cultural and political center. In the Near Eastern world which surrounded Israel, empires in Egypt, Assyria and Babylonia vied for power and prestige. After the allied forces of Egypt and Asyria failed in their attempt to conquer Babylonia, the Babylonians, with Nebuchadnezzar as their king, became the preeminent regional power. They controlled the trade routes from the Persian Gulf to the Mediterranean, amassed enormous wealth and became the overlords of numerous cities and peoples. It was this Babylonian superpower headed by Nebuchadnezzar which employed its army to conquer Jerusalem and destroy the Temple on the ninth day of the Hebrew month of Av (commemorated as *Tisha B'av*). With the destruction of Jerusalem began the period of Jewish history known as the Babylonian Exile. The Jews who survived the Babylonian onslaught were taken in humiliation to Babylon. There, with time, they were able to build a vibrant Jewish community and were, to a great degree, afforded the ability to conduct their religious and communal lives with a good deal of social independence.

Some fifty years after the beginning of the Babylonian Exile, King Darius of Media and King Cyrus of Persia embarked on a campaign which sought to subdue much of the Near and Middle East, including Babylonia. Shortly after Babylonia fell, Cyrus became the king of the entire Persian-Mede empire, and as such inherited the Jews of Babylonia as his subjects. Having been slaves in ancient Egypt, sovereign in Israel during the First Temple period, defeated and exiled by the Babylonians, the Jews were now subject to the rule of one of the greatest empires ever to appear on the stage of history — that of the Persians. It would be that empire and those kings, Cyrus and his successor Achashverosh, who would provide the stage, setting and landscape upon which the story of Purim took place.

3

THE BOOK OF ESTHER: OUTLINE AND OVERVIEW OF THE MEGILLAH

Chapter I. *King Achashverosh Throws A Party.*

1. A lavish 187-day celebration marks the third year in the reign of Achashverosh , king of Persia.
2. Queen Vashti refuses the king's request to appear at the celebration and display her beauty for the assembled guests.
3. The king's advisors counsel that Vashti be replaced with a new queen.

Chapter II. *Esther Becomes The Queen.*

1. Across the Persian Empire officials are appointed to identify beautiful candidates to succeed Vashti as queen.
2. A Jewish girl, Esther, the niece of Mordecai, is brought to the capitol of Persia as one of the candidates.
3. Mordecai tells Esther to conceal her identity.
4. Esther is chosen to be the queen.

5. Mordecai learns of a plot to overthrow the king. Mordecai informs Esther, Esther tells the king and the plotters are hung.

Chapter III. *The Rise Of Haman.*

1. Achashverosh appoints Haman to be his prime minister; all bow in homage to Haman.
2. Mordecai consistently refuses to bow to Haman.
3. An enraged Haman vows to kill all the Jews of Persia.
4. Haman prevails upon Achashverosh to destroy the Jews.
5. A royal edict is disseminated throughout Persia. The thirteenth of Adar is designated as the date to exterminate all the Jews and plunder their possessions.

Chapter IV. *Esther's Mission Becomes Clear.*

1. Mordecai tears his clothes and puts on sackcloth and ashes as a sign of public mourning.
2. Mordecai sends a copy of the decree to Esther and asks her to intercede with the king.
3. Esther replies that to approach the king without being summoned is to risk death.
4. Mordecai tells her that she has no choice.
5. Esther tells Mordecai to ask the Jews to fast and pray for three days before she will approach the king.

Chapter V. *Esther's Strategy — Haman's Fury.*

1 King Achashverosh receives Esther and grants her virtually any request.
2. Esther's request: that the king and Haman join her at a banquet.[1]
3. After the banquet, Haman sees Mordecai who once again refuses to bow.
   a. Haman tells his wife and sons that despite an invitation to a second banquet the next day, the sight of Mordecai clouds his enjoyment.

---

[1]The next two and a half chapters take place within a period of just twenty-four hours.

b. Zeresh, Haman's wife, suggests that Mordecai be hung.

4. The gallows are prepared.

Chapter VI. *The Reversal Begins.*

1. The king can't sleep and asks that the royal chronicles be read to him.

   a. For the first time the king learns of the plot that Mordecai had revealed.

2. That same night Haman comes to see the king about hanging Mordecai.

3. Before Haman can speak, the king tells Haman to honor Mordecai by dressing him in royal garments, placing him on a royal stallion and to personally lead Mordecai through the streets of Shushan, capitol of Persia.

Chapter VII.   *Reversal Of Fortune.*

1. At the second banquet, Esther reveals her identity and announces that she and her people are about to be murdered.

2. Esther identifies Haman as her arch enemy.

3. The king has Haman hung on the gallows that had been prepared for Mordecai.

Chapter VIII. *The Reversal Is Complete.*

1. Mordecai is named prime minister to replace Haman.

2. A second royal edict is promulgated empowering the Jews to fight and kill anyone who would try to harm them.

Chapter IX. *The Holiday Of Purim.*

1. On the thirteenth of Adar, a day that had been designated for Jewish destruction, the Jews are victorious over their enemies.

2. The ten sons of Haman are hung.

3. The fourteenth and fifteenth of Adar are designated to celebrate the salvation. These are the days of Purim.

   a. Mordecai initiates the Purim practices consisting of a festive meal, the exchange of gifts of food and the giving of monetary gifts to the poor.

Chapter X. *Mordecai And Persia.*
1. Persia, with Mordecai as prime minister, flourishes.
2. The role of Mordecai in the history of the Persian empire is recorded in the king's chronicles.

REVERSAL OF FORTUNE

The story of Purim as told in the Book of Esther is the firsthand account of a turn of events which constituted a dramatic reversal of fortune for the Jewish people. The Book of Esther was written by Mordecai and Esther, two of the three central figures in the story. The third player in this real-life drama is Haman. Haman is a man whose hatred for the Jewish people fueled his meteoric rise to power in the court of King Achashverosh, and who sought to use the leverage of his position to bring about the extermination of all the Jews in the Persian Empire. In the end, it was a combination of Mordecai's wisdom, Esther's courage and G-d's subtle and consistent support which saved Persian Jewry from the closing jaws of a hate-driven leadership and an all too willing population of accomplices.

A Layered Turn of Events

True, on the face of things we find an astonishing turn of events. Haman's rise to power is the impetus behind a royal decree granting the citizenry of Persia the freedom to rise up and slaughter their Jewish neighbors. Yet, unbeknownst to Haman and Achashverosh, the king's own wife, Esther, is a Jew. At just the right moment, Esther deftly plays her hand. She reveals the truth of her identity, fingers Haman as the would-be henchman prepared to annihilate her and her people, and wins the king's favor. Esther's interceding leads to the execution of Haman and a second royal decree enabling the Jews of Persia to be saved.

At the same time that these events were unfolding, another reversal was also taking place. The Book of Esther opens with the description of a lavish one-hundred-and-eighty-day feast which King Achashverosh hosted, "for all his officials and servants, the army of Persia and Media, the nobility and provincial officials". This feast culminated in a final week of festivities "for all the people who were present in Shushan the capitol[1], the aristocracy and the commoner alike." But this feast was more than an ancient precursor to Mardi Gras. The Talmud informs us that there was a poignant theme to this party which struck at the heart of Jewish identity and consciousness. This feast not only marked the third anniversary of the reign of King Achashverosh, it also marked seventy years since the destruction of the Temple in Jerusalem. Achashverosh was keenly aware that the Jewish prophets had foretold the end of the Babylonian and Persian exile after seventy years.

Achashverosh miscalculated the precise time when the seventy years began and drew the mistaken conclusion that the Jews would now languish in utter despair, and that the land of Israel and the once glorious Jewish nation would become permanent gems in his own crown of glory. To celebrate the certitude of his dominion over the Jews, Achashverosh staged an elaborate party where he donned the priestly garments plundered from the Temple. Likewise, the uniquely beautiful Temple vessels, which were a part of the Persian treasury, were proudly displayed for all to see. And of course, Achashverosh invited the Jews. And they came, and they enjoyed the celebration. But how could they? Was this feast not the equivalent of a theme park being built on the site of Auschwitz, and inviting Jews to come and enjoy the attractions? True, when the king extends an invitation you can't say no. But enjoy the experience! How?

Somehow, in a relatively short period of time, Jews had become desensitized to the meaning of their history. On some level, the Jews of Persia had lost sight of where they came from and what they

---

[1]Shushan was home to the largest Jewish community in Persia.

could again achieve. So they accepted the mediocrity of the present. Their memories faded and with them a critical degree of sensitivity and commitment. They participated in the feast — and
enjoyed themselves.

Then came Haman, and the threat of annihilation. Again the
Talmud informs us of another dimension to the turn of historical
events. It seems that the imminence of Haman's intentions were the
catalyst for a reawakening of Jewish sensitivities.[1] After all, the
spark which ignited Haman's fury was a confrontation with
"Mordecai the Jew." For after Haman was elevated to his position
of power, everyone in the kingdom "would bow down and prostrate themselves before Haman." To enhance the homage paid to
himself, Haman wore the image of a deity around his neck. This
calculated step leant a religious significance to the ceremonious
bowing. Yet there was one person who bowed to no men and who
acknowledged no deities. This was Mordecai, "and Mordecai
would not bow down or prostrate himself." And since Mordecai
was a Jew, Haman ranted against all the Jews, "And Haman sought
to kill all the Jews, the people of Mordecai, who were in the kingdom of Achashverosh." And when he sought to sell his plan for the
final solution of the Jews in Persia to the king, Haman had only to
point to their Jewishness: "Their laws are different from every other
peoples'."

Beneath the surface, the Book of Esther is about an era in which
the sensitivity of Jews to their own Jewishness was on the wane.
Ironically, there arose at that same juncture an enemy who hated the
Jews specifically because of their Jewishness. And, as the Talmud
goes on to tell us, the Jewish response to their enemy was not to run
from the scourge of their Jewish identity, but to realize that nothing
in the world was more precious to them than their very Jewishness.
So as we reach the end of the Megillah, we find the words, "The
Jews had light and joy, gladness and honor." The sages in the
Talmud tell us that these words not only represent a reaction to the
downfall of Haman but are a reference to a renewal of their com-

---

[1]Talmud, Megillah 14a

mitment to being Jews.[1] Light represents a fresh commitment to studying the wisdom of the Torah. Joy, gladness and honor represent a reinvigorated attachment to the holidays and other observances like circumcision and the wearing of tefillin. The Jews of Persia had now come full circle. Where once they were so casual about their Jewishness that they could enjoy a party celebrating their own physical and spiritual downfall, now events had brought about a fresh appreciation of Jewish life.

On the surface, the story of the Jews in Persia could have been about any people who escaped near annihilation at the hands of their Persian hosts. Yet, aided by the vision of our sages, we are able to see that beneath the surface lays the story of a uniquely Jewish struggle to maintain a passionate sense of identity amidst a host culture that was at times welcoming and, at times, threatening. When Jewish lives were threatened specifically because they were *Jewish* lives, the Jews of Persia realized that not only did they want to live, but more than anything else they wanted to live as Jews.

---

[1]Talmud, Megillah 16b.

4

FIVE QUESTIONS PEOPLE ASK ABOUT PURIM

(I)

Question: Why do people wear costumes on Purim?

Answer: The concept of wearing clothing other than one's own, and of concealing one's identity, is a recurrent theme throughout the story of Purim. In fact, the origins of this idea predate the events of Purim itself. The Talmud asks a strange question:"Where is there an allusion to Esther in the Torah?" A strange question because the Torah was written almost a thousand years before Esther lived. The Talmud answers by quoting the verse, "And I [G-d] will surely hide my face."(Deut. 31:18). The Hebrew word used in the verse for *hide,* is *esther.* The name Esther literally means to hide or to conceal. And isn't that the purpose of a costume, to hide one's face?

Examples of hidden identity and costumes in the story of Purim:

1) When Esther and all the other candidates to become queen were brought to the palace, they were given their choice of clothing, jewelry and make-up to wear when they presented themselves to the king.

2) After being chosen as queen, Esther concealed her identity as a Jew.
3) Mordecai's identity as the one who saved the king's life was hidden from the king until just the right moment.
4) King Achashverosh ordered Haman to dress Mordecai in royal garments and parade him through the streets of Shushan.
5) Haman's identity as the would-be murderer of the king's wife was hidden even from Haman himself.

Insight :   **I. Costumes and Clothing**

People tend to be exceptionally careful about the clothing they wear. After all, who isn't aware that clothing makes a definite statement about who we are? Likewise, we understand that clothing is only one form of adornment. By belonging to particular clubs or groups or organizations we also adorn ourselves. Our affiliations and associations make a statement about who we are. So, too, our furniture, our cars and the magazines we subscribe to. All are outer manifestations of our inner selves.

On Purim we radically alter our most fundamental form of outer expression. We replace our regular clothing with a costume. In so doing we hope not to exchange one costume for another, but to penetrate beneath the outer layers and discover a hidden essence. On Purim we dress as someone we could never be — a king, a queen or even as Haman the Jew hater. Stripped of our usual attire, no longer able to rely on the externalities of clothing to define us, we are free to explore a very personal inner world. Masquerading has a paradoxical way of allowing us to see who we really are. By putting on a face that is not — and never could be — mine, I am able to look within and ask myself, who then am I?

> *Were we to take as much pain to be what*
> *we ought, as we do to disguise what we are,*
> *we might appear like ourselves without*
> *being at the trouble of any disguise at all.*
>
> Francois de la Rochefoucauld

II. Costumes and Laughter

We all have an alter ego, a part of us that would like to be something we are not. This alter ego is an inner adversary that would only foil our best attempts at becoming who it is we want to become and achieving what it is we want to achieve. At times it seems that we are forever locked in a struggle: us against ourselves.

My teacher, Rabbi Noah Weinberg of Jerusalem, used to tell us that on Purim we should dress up as our alter ego. And laugh. You want to devote your weekends to bettering your community but you feel like going fishing. Then dress like a fisherman, and laugh at yourself. You want to be there when your kids need you, but you feel like watching a good movie on television. So dress like a couch potato, and laugh.

Laughter comes when a predictable sequence of events suddenly produces the unexpected. You order a piece of pie for dessert and the waitress gives it to you — right in the face. Ha, ha, ha. Two of you are walking down the street and one of you suddenly trips — ha, ha, ha.

There is also another side to laughter. It cuts things down to size. We have all been witness to the cruelty of a group of children mocking a lone child. How crushed and small that child must feel. At the same time there can be a constructive side to this dimension of laughter — like when we get too serious about things or overly absorbed in our work, or ourselves. At these times, laughter is therapeutic. It cuts things down to size and helps us gain some much needed perspective.

Haman built a gallows upon which to hang Mordecai, and suddenly Haman himself is hung on those very gallows. The thirteenth day of Adar had been decreed as a day of destruction for the Jewish people; and in a flash it became a moment of salvation. Purim is a time for tapping into the power of laughter. We realize that no matter how bleak things seem, we must never give up hope. And when we dress like our alter ego, like a couch potato, a beauty queen or president of the United States — we laugh — and cut our nemesis down to size.

III. Costumes and Freedom. . . From Fear

There is no fear as debilitating as the fear of "what will people think?" We become stifled and stilted when we just can't allow ourselves to be ourselves. All because we are afraid of what people will think.

In this vein, a costume can be liberating. All you need is a mask and some old clothing and no one will ever know who you are. Suddenly you are free to be yourself. You can go around telling corny jokes and making people laugh, if bringing smiles to people's faces is what you would really like to do. Or you can spend time visiting a nursing home, if warming lonely hearts is what you are really all about. Or you can be a king and treat your wife like a queen. Or a horse and give all the neighborhood kids a ride. Or anything else you really want to be, but aren't, because of what other people will think. And, if you do it right on Purim, you just might find that you no longer care as much, about what other people think.

(II)

Question: Where does the name of the holiday – Purim – come from?

Answer: When Haman wanted to choose a date to execute his planned destruction of the Jews, he engaged in the practice of "casting lots" to determine the most auspicious time. The casting of lots was a type of astrological device used to predict the nature of particular dates based on the day, the month and the position of various constellations. The Hebrew word for "lot" (as in lottery) is *pur,* and serves as the basis for the word *Pur*im, which literally means "lots." Haman was a master of these astrological-based arts and discovered that the thirteenth day of the month of Adar was well-suited to his plans. A close look at the text of the Megillah reveals that "a lot *(pur)* was cast in the presence of Haman." Haman himself did not cast the lots, rather some unknown character did it for him.

This ancient role of the dice is the veneer of history. A faceless hand, an arbitrary flick-of-the-wrist and suddenly hundreds of thousands of Jews are scheduled to die. How cold the irrational whims of history seem to be. How utterly meaningless.

Still, even in the face of countless horrors, the Jewish people live on. And as we live, we thrive, and as we thrive, we do so with dignity and honor; proud and grateful to be Jews. What is the secret of our perseverance? We reject an arbitrary reading of history. No, we don't pretend to understand everything that happens. Yet we shun both cynicism and despair when we can't read the headlines on the tragic events that dot our history.

On Monday, October 10th, 1994, the Israeli public was informed that Nachshon Waxman had been captured by Hamas terrorists. By Friday he was dead.

During the shiva (seven day mourning period), rabbis, politicians and army generals all emerged from their visits with Nachshon's parents – Yehuda and Esther Waxman – with the same sentiments. "We came to comfort and strengthen the Waxmans, instead, we were comforted and strengthened by them."

Ask anyone who was there that week and they will tell you that the Waxmans were able to emotionally unite the people of Israel to a degree it hadn't felt for years. Yehuda and Esther are both religious children of holocaust survivors. He grew up in Rumania and she in Flatbush. They met, married and settled in Israel. As parents, they raised their sons to be devout and learned Jews, loyal and courageous soldiers.

During the week of the kidnapping, the Waxmans appealed to all of Israel to transform their country into one massive synagogue; and everyone responded. For a week the entire country seemed to stand silent in prayer. Each morning the newspapers printed a notice indicating the special prayers that were to be recited that day. Each day schools across the country set aside time to pray for Nachshon. Each day synagogues that had few regular visitors during the week were packed for hours on end.

A friend of mine was in a cab in Jerusalem that week. The secular Israeli cab driver handed him a prayer book —"I can't pray while I'm driving," he said, "but you can." The Yediot Achronot, one of Israels largest daily newspapers wrote that "An entire secular country prayed in the depths of its heart for the rescue of Nachshon Waxman." Late on Friday afternoon, shortly before the country was sent reeling from the news of Nachshon's death, hundreds of thousands of women responded to Esther Waxman's request to light an extra Shabbat candle for Nachshon.

In the end, Esther comforted her people, "Prayers don't get lost," she said, "Jews prayed for 2,000 years to return to Israel. Our generation made it back. Eventually the time comes for the fulfillment of prayers."

What does it take to respond with dignity in the face of horrible tragedies? Some would say that all it takes is the blind faith of a simpleton. Yehuda and Esther Waxman in our time, like Mordecai and Esther in their time, showed us that what it really takes is courage. The courage to believe in the Jewish people and the Jewish dream. That one day the veneer of history will crumble, that prayers will be answered, and that goodness will ultimately prevail.

(III)

Question: Why do we read the Megillah on Purim?

Answer: The Megillah, the Book of Esther, is read twice on Purim. Once at night when the holiday begins and again in the morning before a full day of festivities get underway. The holiday of Purim is a celebration of the miraculous salvation of the Jews of Persia from what seemed to be certain death. The events recorded in the Megillah are the story of how the Jews were saved.

The reading of the Megillah provides a historical and intellectual context in which we carry out the Purim celebration. The Megillah is known for its subtlety and many layers of meaning. For this reason, it is helpful to study the Megillah prior to Purim. The greater our understanding, the more fulfilling the holiday becomes.

Insight: There is an old saying, "Experience is the best teacher." While there is truth in this notion, if accepted uncritically, this old adage can be down right dangerous.

It's true, the best way to learn to fill a cavity is to fill a cavity. But not before you've entered dental school! Likewise; don't set sail without first learning the difference between the bow and the stern; don't get married without learning the difference between love and romance, and don't expect to appreciate a holiday before learning about the central themes and ideas which permeate the holiday.

Purim is a complex holiday — meals and gifts, synagogue and *shpiels* (skits), parties, costumes and a lot more. We begin both the night and the day of Purim by reading the Megillah in order to focus on the meaning our celebration is meant to express. Far more than a Jewish Halloween, Purim is rich in insight, symbolism and spirituality, all of which have their source in the Megillah. Study it, consider its implications, discuss it with others — and then — party like you've never partied before; with your mind, heart and eyes wide open.

(IV)

Question: Why do some people get drunk on Purim?

Answer: The *Shulchan Aruch* (the legal code of Jewish living) states that "A person is required to get spiced [drunk] on Purim to the extent of not being able to distinguish between cursed is Haman and blessed is Mordecai." No mincing of words here. When they say that an appropriate part of the Purim festivities is to have a drink — they mean HAVE A DRINK!

Insight: The Talmud makes two pithy statements about the potential affects that alcohol can have on a person: 1) "You can tell what people are all about by observing them when they drink" and 2) "When the wine goes in, the secrets come out."

When a person has had "one too many" drinks there is no telling what might come out. Aren't we then asking for trouble when we encourage spirited drinking on Purim? And what's more, can you imagine anything less Jewish then mandating drunkenness, and on a holiday no less?

The requirement to drink on Purim must be understood within the broader context of Jewish life. The same Jewish corpus of laws, ethics and commandments which mandates visiting the sick, fasting on Yom Kippur, lighting candles on Friday night and honoring one's parents also calls upon us to "get spiced" on Purim.

> *Man is at bottom a wild and terrible animal...whenever the locks and chains of law and order are cast off and anarchy comes in, he shows himself for what he really is.*
> Schopenhauer

One of the primary functions of Jewish life is to refine the human character: To spiritualize that which is physical, humanize that which would be animal and civilize that which would be savage. History has well acquainted us with humankind's potential for corruption, evil and debauchery. While Judaism recognizes the dark side of human potential, its aim is to champion everything noble that a human being can become.

The word *Torah* literally means instructions. In our daily prayers we refer to the Torah as *Torat chaim — Instructions for living.* When Jewish law mandates drinking on Purim, it is the ultimate expression of confidence in the goodness of human potential and in the ability of Jewish instructions to nurture that potential.

The Torah well understands what dread may be unleashed by a man caught in the grips of too much drink. But on Purim it has no such fears, because drinking on Purim is drinking in the context of Jewish moral and spiritual living. In such a setting, Jewish law anticipates that when one's inhibitions are melted away, what will be revealed are new layers of care, compassion, spirituality and joy.

Note: Jewish law blends the idealistic and the practical. For those who are genuinely concerned about what may come out if they drink too much, the law suggests that they have a small drink and then take a nap. Once asleep, they too will be unable to distinguish between Haman and Mordecai.

(V)

Question: What is the purpose of the *gragger*, the Purim noisemaker?

Answer: The reading of the Megillah on Purim is an event in the life of every synagogue when there appears to be a general breakdown in decorum. Barely a paragraph goes by without the incoherent wail of untold noisemakers interrupting the rabbi and drowning out his best efforts to read from the sacred parchment scroll.

A close observation reveals that there is a particular word in the text of the Megillah which triggers the clamorous response from the outrageously clad Purim worshippers. The word is Haman. While Haman is the villain of the Purim story, in truth, he represents far more than one regime's attempt to destroy the Jewish people. Haman is a descendent of the Jewish nation's arch enemy, the people of Amalek. Ever since the Amalakite's first unprovoked attack on the Jews, after their receiving the Torah at Mt. Sinai, Amalek and their descendants have been identified as the classical champions of evil, and the Jewish people's existential rival. Ominously, over two hundred years before the rise of modern Germany, in reference to a passage in the Talmud, two great Jewish scholars identified the region inhabited by the German tribes as the locale of this era's descendants of Amalek.[1]

The Torah assigns a particular commandment to "erase" any memory of the nation of Amalek. By making noise when Haman's name is mentioned during the Megillah reading, we are symbolically erasing the name of Haman and thereby blotting out the memory of Amalek.

Insight: **1)** Synagogue is serious and solemn; a place for reflection, study, prayer and FUN! For Jewish kids whose parents only take them to synagogue twice a year, I would like to cast a vote in favor of those two days being Purim and Simchat Torah, not Rosh Hashanah and Yom Kippur. When children—and adults— immerse themselves in the celebration of Purim, one of the most important lessons they learn is that Jewish life incorporates the gamut of human emotional experience. Singing and dancing, costumes, fun and all around merrymaking are as integral to Judaism as charity, prayer and fasting.

2) Judaism believes in identifying evil for what it is — evil. While people readily acknowledge certain *actions* as evil, they are loathe to label the perpetrators of those actions as evil.

Is a systematic attempt to exterminate an entire group of people whose only crime is their identification with a common religious ancestry evil? Of course it is. Everyone admits that. But what about the individuals who carefully calculated, planned and implemented

---

[1]See Talmud, Tractate Megillah 6b. Commentary of Rabbi Yaacov Emden (1695-1776) and Rabbi Eliyahu of Vilna (1720-1797). More contemporary Jewish thinkers like Rabbi Joseph B. Soloveitchik zt"l, contend that anyone who tries to destroy the Jewish people simply because they are Jews are to be considered as the heirs to the mantle of Amalek.

every detail of the extermination of a people who posed no territorial or military threat? Are those people evil or are they just sick?

Judaism does not deny the existence of individuals with the most extreme psychological disorders, but it does assert that one need not be "sick" to carry out the most brutal and hideous of crimes. Adolf Hitler, Adolf Eichmann and the thousands of doctors, professors, farmers, teachers, barbers, receptionists, retailers, lawyers, mechanics, entrepreneurs and secretaries who made soap, lamp shades, coat stuffing and ashes out of Jews were not sick! They were just plain evil.

The *gragger* in the hand of a child on Purim is there to remind us how to relate to evil. Like Amalek, it must be erased. Not by labeling it as sick and psychoanalyzing it into oblivion, but by calling it what it is — evil — and dealing with it as bluntly as it would deal with us.

5

LET'S DO PURIM:
A STEP-BY-STEP GUIDE TO CELEBRATING THE HOLIDAY

I. The Month of Adar: Prelude to Purim

The holiday of Purim is celebrated in the middle of the Hebrew month of Adar. In actuality, Purim begins long before it starts. The Talmud tells us "with the onset of Adar it is appropriate to increase the feeling of joy." The joyous celebration of Purim is to be preceded by a two-week period during which we make a conscious effort to expand our capacity for experiencing joy in life.

Jumping for Joy

Joy is an emotional state of being in which we recognize that life is a pleasure. To experience joy is to experience the goodness in life — the feeling that "it's great to be alive" and, at the same time, to confidently anticipate that the future will also be a time of pleasure. Joy is one part of our emotional reality. It is realistic and never deludes us into denying life's bitter pills. Rather, it is a state of inner celebration which comes from focusing on life's bounty of blessings, both large and small — the blessings of today, and those which are yet to be.

Jewish thought views joy as being a state which is dependent more on our attitudes towards events than on the nature of events themselves. While there are events which certainly produce a spontaneous burst of joy, the ability to incorporate the feeling of joy as a permanent thread in the fabric of our personalities is almost solely dependent on the efforts we make to *acquire* this trait. The Hebrew word for joy is *simcha*. When it comes to living life with *simcha*, with joy, classical Jewish texts are replete with ideas and techniques which can be used to "increase the feeling of joy" — as Purim approaches, and throughout our lives. The following is a sampling of techniques that can be used to increase joy and achieve a sense of inner celebration.

1) Fake it! In other words, identify a particular time or setting in which you don't anticipate feeling joyous and act like you're feeling it anyway. By choosing to model joyful behavior superficially, you will find that with time, the feeling will begin to seep into the recesses of your character and become a part of the real you —and no longer be just a role you are playing. As Thomas Watson said, *If you want to be a big company tomorrow, you have to start acting like one today.*

2) Every night at dinner (or as often as possible) ask everyone at the table to share one moment when they felt joy that day. An alternative to this is to share "something that I felt grateful for today." Where there is gratitude, joy is rarely far behind.

3) Count your blessings. At the beginning of the month of Adar make a list of ten things you are grateful for — ten blessings in your life. Every day until Purim add another blessing to your list. Then, on a regular basis, read this list to yourself. When you finish read-

ing, choose one blessing and articulate the specific ways in which this blessing enhances your life.

4) Go to a Jewish bookstore (or call 1-800-JUDAISM) and buy a children's tape about Purim that includes music and songs. Listen to it on the way to work — really loud — with the windows closed of course. A secret: the joy begins when you start singing along.

5) Think about why you are glad to be a Jew. To take it one step further, ask yourself, "Now that I've lived for 'x' number of years, if I could go back in time and control my destiny, would I choose to be born a Jew?" If you're glad you're a Jew — feel it!

6) Go out of your way to bring someone else joy. You will be amazed how much joy this will bring into your own life.

7) Trust G-d. Nourish yourself spiritually by developing the aspect of trust in your relationship with G-d. Focus on the times when you felt G-d was at your side helping and watching over you. See how many of your blessings can be traced back to yourself and how many go back to G-d. Now, begin to count on G-d's involvement and assistance as you strive to direct your life in a meaningful and pleasurable direction. When you sense that G-d is a partner in your life, you will become aware of a new dimension of joy.

8) For daring joy-seekers only: DANCE! With your spouse, with your kids, with a friend or even by yourself. Dance and sing out loud.

II. The Fast of Esther: One Day Before Purim

The thirteenth of Adar, one day before Purim, is a fast day. This is not a full twenty-four hour fast like Yom Kippur, rather it is a minor fast which begins at sunrise and concludes with sunset.[1] At

---

[1] While the Fast of Esther is an obligatory observance, it is less stringent than the fast on Yom Kippur. This is particularly relevant to someone who is ill and for pregnant or nursing mothers. Specific cases and questions regarding fasting should be directed to a rabbi.

the same time that the Fast of Esther *(Ta'anis Esther)* is ending, the time for reading the Megillah arrives. For this reason, it is customary for many synagogues to have refreshments available after the Megillah reading for people who haven't eaten all day.

It's Not the Fast You Think it is

Mordecai called upon Queen Esther to approach the king on behalf of the Jews of Persia. Esther agreed, but asked that the Jews first fast for three days before she would approach the king. The purpose of this fast was to focus every ounce of Jewish attention on the fact that while Esther would approach one king, the course of Jewish history is ultimately guided by another king: namely, G-d himself.

This three-day fast was an integral part of the turn of events recorded in the Megillah. That fast, however, is not the fast we commemorate on the day before Purim. The three-day fast took place in the Hebrew month of Nissan (when Passover occurs) and the fast that we observe today is on the thirteenth of Adar. Why then do we fast on the thirteenth of Adar, the day before Purim, and why is it called the "Fast of Esther" if it's not the fast which Esther initiated?

Of War and Fasting

There are few things more powerful than a person with a sense of mission. A group of citizens who have banded together to search for a lost child, a candidate on the campaign trail, or a soldier behind enemy lines. Each of these has the ability to dispense with their usual need for food and sleep in order to achieve what they have set out to achieve. Each is able to do without their standard ration of fuel because each has discovered an alternative source of energy. Their missions drive their spirits further than calories could ever drive their bodies. Kind of like being a devoted parent — only easier.

Fasting attunes us to our soul. The soul is the seat of our life's mission and serves as our personal nuclear reactor. The inner voice that tells you to go back and apologize — that's your soul. That part of you that says to listen to your spouse with your fullest attention and concern, despite the difficulty of your day — that's your soul. The more aligned we are with the ways of our soul, the more driven and resourceful we become. We all possess the power of drivenness. It's the energy necessary to build healthy relationships as well as the energy needed to build a healthy world.

But it doesn't end there. Because the more attuned and connected we become to our soul, the more connected we become to G-d.

> *Concerning all acts of initiative and creation, there is one elementary truth, the ignorance of which kills countless ideas and splendid plans: that the moment one definitely commits oneself, then Providence moves too. All sorts of things occur to help one that would never otherwise have occurred.*
>
> W.H. Murray
> The Scottish Himalayan Expedition

And that is why we fast on the thirteenth of Adar. Besides the three-day fast which Esther called for, there was another one-day fast which took place on Adar the thirteenth. The thirteenth of Adar was originally slated as a day for Jewish destruction. A second decree enabled the Jews to wage war against their attackers on that same day. And, before the Jews went out to war, they fasted. Fasting focused them on their souls, on G-d and on the meaning and significance of Jewish survival. Rather than grow weary, the fast galvanized their will and fueled the victory. It is this fast, and this idea, which we identify with each year.

The Esther in Each of Us

We are left with one final question. Why do we call the fast on the day before we celebrate Purim the Fast of Esther — who was an individual – when this fast commemorates a group effort? The answer must lay in the truth of the assertion that "a chain is only as strong as its weakest link." The Jewish people are a spiritual chain which stretches from Abraham down through the time of Esther to our very day. The strength of that chain depends on the strength —the moral and spiritual fortitude — of each and every one of us.

III. The Day of Purim

This section will discuss the five primary observances which take place on Purim. Each of the five will be addressed on four levels: What, How, When and Why. (Note: I. This is not meant to be a definitive book on Jewish law. Specific questions relating to the observance of Purim should be directed to someone familiar with the relevant source texts. II. When we address the Why of the observances we are only offering a sampling of the deeper meaning that lays beneath these *mitzvot* (commandments). Further study is always appropriate.)

The five observances are: 1) The reading of the *Megillah,* the Book of Esther, 2) The special prayer of *Al Ha-nisim,* "for the miracles", 3) *Mishloach Manot,* gifts of food, 4) *Matanot L'evyonim,* gifts of money for the poor, and 5) *Seudat Purim,* the Purim meal.

1) The Reading of the Megillah.

WHAT: One must hear the Megillah being read twice on Purim.

HOW: Attend a synagogue where the entire Megillah will be read aloud in Hebrew. One must follow the reading carefully and listen to every word. If you can't read Hebrew, that's okay, do the best you can to listen. Whether you understand Hebrew or not, it will be very helpful to familiarize yourself with the story ahead of time.

WHEN: The Megillah is read twice — once at night when Purim begins and again the next morning. If, due to sickness, hospitalization or other causes one is unable to attend synagogue, there are usually volunteer Megillah readers who make the rounds so everyone can hear the Megillah. If you know someone who is ill, it is advisable to call local synagogues before Purim to find out who in your city provides this service.

WHY: In Hebrew the Megillah is known as *Megillat Esther*, the scroll of Esther. The word *megillah*, in addition to its literal meaning, scroll, also means to *reveal*. The word *esther* literally means *hidden*. Together they convey one of Purim's central themes, *to reveal that which is hidden*. On the surface, the story of Purim is just another recollection of ancient historical events. Beneath the surface, "coincidence" after "coincidence" pile one on top of the other to reveal the presence of G-d in Jewish history.

The Book of Esther is unique amongst all the books of the Torah, Prophets and Writings (the *Tanach*), in that it is the only book in which G-d's name never appears. Tradition has it that whenever the text says "King Achashverosh," this is a historical reference to the king himself, but when a verse only says "The King," this not only refers to Achashverosh but is an allusion to the presence of G-d in the story. The Megillah sensitizes us to a dimension of reality in history, and in ourselves, which often goes overlooked.

2) The Prayer of *Al Ha-nisim*, "For the Miracles."

WHAT: During the daily prayers when one recites the *Amidah* (the silent or standing prayer), and also in *Birkat Hamazon*, the blessing after eating a meal, one must be careful to insert the special paragraph of *Al Ha-nisim*. This paragraph contains a brief summary of the miracle of Purim.

HOW: Purim is a wonderful time to attend synagogue. When else can you witness Batman praying or get Queen Esther's autograph? In synagogue, look through the prayerbook for special instructions of when to say *Al Ha-nisim.* If you can't find it, just ask the cowboy next to you.

WHEN: This prayer can be said at least four times. During the evening, morning, and afternoon prayer service and at the conclusion of the festive Purim meal.

WHY: Prayer is a means by which we develop our relationship with G-d. Like other relationships, this one is full of subtlety and even hesitancy. It also becomes deeper with time. Every Jewish holiday presents us with a unique dimension of our relationship with G-d. The *Al Ha-nisim* prayer highlights the uniqueness of Purim.

3) *Mishloach Manot:* Sending Gifts of Food.

WHAT: All men and women are obligated to send at least one gift of food to another person on Purim.

HOW: 1) This gift of food, commonly referred to as *shaloch manos*, must consist of at least two types of food that are ready to be eaten, i.e., that require no cooking. 2) Each individual must appoint a representative to present the gift to the recipient on behalf of the sender.

WHEN: This takes place during the day of Purim. Though the minimum requirement is to send one gift to one person, it is quite common for individuals and families to send numerous gifts to friends and neighbors. For this reason, many people spend a number of hours on Purim afternoon traveling their neighborhood in all sorts of costumes, while delivering all sorts of luscious gifts.

WHY: The sending of *shaloch manos* is a vehicle to spur feelings of camaraderie and unity amongst Jews. *Mishloach manot*, the sending of food gifts, is a mitzvah with a radical message. While war, terrorism and impending crisis seem to be effective catalysts for Jewish solidarity, *mishloach manot* says, there has got to be a better way.

The Meaning of Jewish Unity

Before Esther would approach the king on behalf of the Jews she told Mordecai, "Go and gather together all the Jews." Esther knew that Jewish unity and Jewish survival go hand in hand.

Jewish solidarity is not optional for the Jewish people. The existence of the Jewish people is predicated on our unity; a unity that expresses itself as the full-fledged mutual responsibility of brotherhood.

Our sages teach us that just prior to the receiving of the Torah at Mt. Sinai, the Jewish people achieved a degree of unity which they characterized as "being like one person with one heart." It is no coincidence that the Jewish people achieved this state of indivisibility at the foot of Mt. Sinai. A profound sense of national harmony was considered to be an essential prerequisite to the giving of the Torah.

Giving; the Gift of Unity

To the contemporary lament of Jewish disunity, Purim offers the following response and suggestion: give gifts. The way to access our latent capacity for expressing the existential reality of Jewish oneness is by being benevolent to one another.

Rabbi Eliyahu E. Dessler[1] a major twentieth century expositor of Jewish thought, taught that when a person chooses to give of themselves to another, whether they are giving a gift of food, time, money or expertise, the very fact of giving draws them closer.

---

[1] See Strive for Truth, vol. 1, pg. 118-130. English translation by Aryeh Carmell, Feldheim Publishers, 1988.

When I give of myself to another, I am, in essence, transferring a part of myself to the recipient. I am planting a bit of my being into the soil of someone else's life. And as we implant bits of ourselves into one another, we are naturally drawn together. We begin to see and care for one another in a new light. As we are aware of ourselves — sensitive and responsive to our own needs — so we become sensitized to the needs of others in whom a portion of ourselves now exists.

On Purim we do more than just *give* gifts, we *send* them with someone who delivers them on our behalf. Why? To highlight the idea that each of us must be ready to serve as a force for facilitating Jewish unity — on Purim, and throughout the year.

4) *Matanot L'evyonim*: Gifts of Money For the Poor.

WHAT: All men and women are obligated to give gifts of money to at least two poor people on Purim.

HOW: If there are poor Jews in your community, then it is a *mitzvah* (a commandment) on Purim to help them financially. These gifts should be over and above any other gifts that would be extended during the year.

WHEN: Ideally these gifts should be distributed on Purim. If you don't know any poor people in your area, it is advisable to locate a synagogue that makes a point of distributing money to poor families on Purim. One can discharge his or her obligation of giving money to the poor on Purim by making a donation to such a fund.

WHY: This beautiful *mitzvah* of giving gifts to the needy not only expresses the mutual concern inherent in Jewish unity, but serves to further engender that feeling as well. The *halacha* (Jewish law), states that on Purim one should give freely and not refuse any poor person who asks for assistance.

It is very easy to get lost in the labyrinth of our own needs and problems. On Purim, for one day, we are asked to set our own needs aside. We learn to lift our eyes and see beyond the burden of our own concerns. As we lift our eyes and allow them to meet the eyes of someone less fortunate than ourselves, as we give — and give freely— we benefit not only the poor, but ourselves and the Jewish people as well.

5) *Seudat Purim* : The Purim Meal.

WHAT: To enjoy a particularly festive meal during the day of Purim. While it is appropriate and common for people to also add a festive quality to their meal on Purim night, there is only an obligation during the day.

HOW: One should serve special foods, delicacies, desserts and the like at this meal. There is a special requirement to drink more wine or liquor at the meal than one is generally accustomed to. For those who are able, the drinking is "until you can't tell the difference between cursed is Haman and blessed is Mordecai." (For a discussion of drunkenness on Purim see page 30). Where there is a chance that too much drinking will lead to inappropriate or dangerous behavior it is certainly preferable not to drink. An alternative to drinking a lot is to have a small amount to drink and then take a nap. Once you are asleep it is also impossible to distinguish between Haman and Mordecai.

WHEN: This meal can take place anytime during the day of Purim. Customarily, the meal is held in the afternoon after one has already fulfilled the *mitzvot* of hearing the Megillah, *mishloach manot* (food gifts) and *matanot l'evyonim* (giving money to the poor). In the spirit of Jewish unity, it is also common to invite guests to this meal. Communal meals are also quite common.

WHY: The Purim meal holds one of the keys to living with a genuine sense of joy. Regarding joy, the Talmud teaches, "There is no joy like the resolution of doubt." Feelings of doubt and uncertainty are some of the greatest causes of tension known to man. Where there are conflicting and competing sides to an issue — should I get married or shouldn't I, should I accept the position or shouldn't I, should we have kids or shouldn't we — there is doubt, hesitancy and tension. Where there is a resolution of doubt, there is harmony, commitment and joy.

Life's most basic conflict, and the source of much of our inner dissonance, is the tension between body and soul, the physical and the spiritual. There is a part of us, our soul, that wants to be patient and compassionate. But the body, ever in search of the easy way out, tugs in another direction. "Let's relax" it says. "It's too hard. . . . It doesn't pay. . . . " Our soul says, "Life is so short. Let's do something meaningful while we can. . . . Lets make a difference. . . . Let's help make this a better world. . . ." But the body has something else in mind. "Gimme a break" it says. "What can one person do? Let's enjoy ourselves while we have the chance. Life is so short you know." In this manner, at times a skirmish while at other times a war, the battle of life rages on. And with it comes tension, clouded vision and the persistent voice of doubt. Doubting whether we should soar with our souls or relax with our bodies; strive to access our potential or continue on cruise control. Doubt, whether to respond to the challenge of our spirituality or capitulate to what our physical urges feel like doing.

Judaism believes that lasting personal growth and joy are to be found in the management of the tension between body and soul. The principal effort required to grow and fully develop ourselves lies in the realm of achieving a harmony between the spiritual and the physical. To this end, we reject self-flagellation, the denigration of our physicality and the denial of genuine physical needs. Instead, we seek partnership not dominance; harmony and not friction.

Physical pleasures, like food, marital intimacy and a day at the beach, are all meaningful, appropriate and even holy when they are pursued as a means and not as an end. Food is not a goal, though neither is it an enemy. Food is a source of vitality which fuels our bodies and provides a pleasant lift that enables us to pursue lasting achievement and meaningful goals — the goals of the soul.

When the soul's vision determines our priorities, and when bodily pleasures are employed to enhance our ability to live in consonance with the soul's agenda, then the dissipation of tension begins. The clouds of doubt are lifted and rays of joy are able to emerge.

The festive Purim meal is a paradigm. It makes the following statement: the body and the soul are capable of walking hand in hand. A day full of *mitzvot* (commandments) and a day full of festivity need not be mutually exclusive. When spirituality creates the context into which physicality is incorporated, the result is a fusion of two superpowers into one energized and joyous alliance. This is a human being at its finest.

6

KUSTOM MADE FOR KIDS (OF ALL AGES)

Every dimension of the Purim holiday offers endless possibilities for creativity and activities which will help children form a strong bond with the holiday. The ideas and suggestions put forth in this chapter represent but a fraction of the fun families can have with Purim.

Looking beyond the fun, it is important for parents to appreciate the statement that their actions and attitudes make. Children who, year in and year out, see their parents "get into" the holiday will learn that Jewish holidays can be a wonderful part of life throughout one's entire life. Children who, year after year, see their parents studying the Megillah of Esther, will learn to value being educated Jews. And children who study and celebrate together with their parents, will learn to study and celebrate together with their children.

I. The Megillah of Esther
Understand Purim and Value Torah Study

1) Know the story well. The Book of Esther is a very short story that can be read in twenty minutes or less. Read it two or three times so that you will be familiar with the story line when you read it together with your kids.

2) The family that studies together stays together. Beginning three to four weeks before Purim, set aside two nights a week to study the megillah with your kids. There are many good books available about Purim which contain commentary and explanation of the megillah. Visit a Jewish bookstore and, depending on your children's ages, choose those books which can serve as references at your study sessions.

   A) What if your kids balk at this idea and complain that they already go to Sunday school or Hebrew school? Solution: those weeks when the family studies together, give them off from Hebrew school. Just tell the teacher what you are doing — they'll understand.

3) Buy each of your children their own megillah to study. When Purim arrives this will also be the Megillah they take to synagogue with them. Again, the specific megillah you buy will need to be appropriate to the age of the child.

4) Discussion questions: Issues of Jewish identity and anti-semitism are both prominent themes in the Megillah. Purim is a good time to bring up these issues for general family discussion. Try discussing one question a night at dinner time during the week before Purim.

   Sample questions:
   1)   Have you ever felt uncomfortable or unaccepted because you were Jewish?
   2)   Make a list of the following items and then score each one

according to how much it contributes to your identity. Each item receives a score of 1-5, with 1 being "contributes significantly to my identity" and 5 being, "makes a minor contribution to my identity."

1. Parents _____ .
2. School _____ .
3. Jewish holidays _____ .
4. Secular holidays (New Year's, Thanksgiving, Halloween, etc.) _____ .
5. Friends _____ .
6. Country _____ .
7. Sports teams _____ .
8. Brothers and sisters _____ .
9. Judaism _____ .
10. Television shows _____ .
11. The books I read _____ .
12. Israel _____ .
13. Grandparents _____ .
14. Movies _____ .
15. Music _____ .

3) Are you proud of being Jewish? If the answer is yes, ask for the reasons why. If the answer is no, ask for the reasons why not.

4) Do you think it could ever become dangerous for Jews to live in America? Why or why not?

5) If it was against the law to celebrate Purim (as it was in the Soviet Union until recently) would you celebrate anyway, risking your job, a large fine, six months in jail or being denied admission to college?

6) Generally speaking, do you think religion is a positive force in the world or a negative one? What about Judaism specifically?

II. Mishloach Manot - Food Gifts
Jewish Unity Begins at Home

1) Your family *shaloch manos* list. Make sure that every child gets to include the friends, neighbors, teachers or classmates they want. You may also want to include some strangers on your list. If there are any elderly people who live alone in your neighborhood, this is a wonderful way to add some joy to their lives. Also, if there are Russian immigrant families in your area, this is a great way to reach out, make contact, and welcome them to the Jewish community. (For logistical or economic reasons it may be necessary to limit the total number of people on the family list and the number which each child can contribute to the list. Parents should make this decision ahead of time.)

2) The contents. Make a list of ten possible items to be included in your *shaloch manos* and allow each child to choose one. By first compiling a master list you can control issues such as cost and nutritional value. Left to their own devices, children will inevitably choose candy, candy, and more candy to fill the *shaloch manos*.

3) Baking. If you decide to include baked goods in your *shaloch manos,* why not get the whole family involved in the baking? (Of course there are many reasons why not, but occasionally it's worth the mess.) And, as long as you are going to make a mess, why not go all the way and find a great recipe for *hamantashen*.[1]

4) The container. My suggestion: keep it simple. A brown lunch bag, which kids can decorate, clear plastic bags tied with colored ribbon, or paper plates wrapped in colored cellophane paper will work just fine.

---

[1] Hamantashen are three-cornered cookies with a poppy seed or fruit filling. The distinct shape is said to represent Haman's triangular hat. In Israel, these cookies are known as *aznei Haman,* Haman's ears.

A) When it comes to *shaloch manos* baskets there is no end to the creative possibilities. At the same time one should keep two things in mind: 1) Cost. It's better to spend less on fancy *shaloch manos* and to use the money for gifts to the poor. 2) Keeping up with the Cohens. This is a *mitzvah* of unity which requires sensitivity. We certainly don't want anyone to be embarrassed because they can't afford to send a lavish *shaloch manos* basket.

B) You can include a standardized note from your family to the recipients. Make photocopies of the note and have the kids decorate them.

5) *Shaloch manos* packing party. This can be planned for a Sunday afternoon before Purim or on the night of Purim when the family returns from hearing the Megillah.

6) Delivery. On Purim afternoon get all the kids dressed in their costumes and devote a couple of hours to driving around and delivering your *shaloch manos*.

III. Costumes and Graggers
It's Time to Let Your Hair Down

1) Costumes are not just for kids. As was discussed earlier on page 23, there is much significance attached to the wearing of costumes on Purim. Clearly, an adult level of awareness and sensitivity is required to fully access the potential within this custom. Additionally, there is nothing quite so healthy as parents and kids dressing up and having a great time together.

2) The easiest way to handle costumes is to go out and buy or rent one. A good costume rental store will have everything from gorillas and knights in shining armor to nuns and creatures from outer space. Go ahead, take the kids. I dare you.

3) Do it yourself. While store-bought is great, there is still nothing like a creative homemade costume. Closets, basements and attics generally have more than one needs to design award winning cos-

tumes. Besides the kings, queens and Mordecai, I've seen kids dressed as a bottle of wine, a Megillah, and a human *hamantashen.*

4) Graggers are not just for kids. Come on mom and dad—let loose—you too can have a blast while drowning out the name of Haman. (see page 31)

5) Sure, you can buy graggers and take them to synagogue with you, or you can use the ready-made graggers you already have at home. Like alarm clocks, toddler xylophones, dolls that cry with the push of a button, a toy police car with siren and flashing lights or anything else that will make a wonderfully annoying noise.

6) A gragger-making art project can also be a lot of fun. Fill a can or plastic cup with beans, glue on a handle, decorate, and presto — homemade madness.

7) So you despise the evil Haman and want to see his name wiped out forever. Great, just write Haman on a piece of masking tape, stick it to the bottom of your shoe and spend the day stamping out Haman. Or write Haman on your napkins, wipe your face or table with him and then toss him into the garbage. Bye, bye, Haman.

IV. Matanot L'evyonim - Gifts for the Poor
Jewish Sensitivity Training for Kids

1) You receive lots of mail requests for Jewish causes that provide assistance for poor families, orphans, immigrants, Israeli hospitals and the like. Put some of these aside and save them for Purim. On or before Purim spend an hour with your kids discussing what the various causes are all about, writing the checks and mailing them. Yes, children of all ages can be cruel and selfish, but they also have hearts of gold. Help them discover their hearts.

2) The Purim *pushke* (charity box). A month before Purim put a can or jar in a special place in the kitchen. Ask everyone in the family, and guests too, to deposit some loose change on a daily basis. A

week or so before Purim, add up the money, write a check and send it to an organization that distributes money on Purim.

3) Fundraiser for a day. Find an organization that distributes funds to needy Jewish families. On Purim, in synagogue and while you deliver your *shaloch manos,* tell people that you are collecting money for poor families and then ask for a donation. Parents and kids can fan out in synagogue to reach as many people as possible.

V. The Purim Meal

1) The Purim trivia game. Based on your studies prior to Purim, make a list of questions. Give everyone at your meal a chance to answer some questions. All correct (or close to correct) answers get a prize. Prizes can include Purim stickers, party favors, candy, or an extra shot of vodka. (To qualify for a prize of shots of vodka one must first deposit his or her car keys with the host.)

Some suggested questions:
1) What was Haman's wife's name?
2) Esther had another name, what was it?
3) Which of the Jewish tribes was Mordecai from?
4) How many sons did Haman have?
5) Who was queen of Persia before Esther?
6) Who was plotting to overthrow King Achashverosh?
7) What did Esther send to Mordecai when he was wearing sackcloth?
8) Who had a problem falling asleep?
9) Achashverosh offered Esther half the kingdom. What did she ask for?
10) How many provinces did Achashverosh rule over?

MISSILES

MASKS AND

MIRACLES

This chapter is an excerpt from the book *Missiles Masks And Miracles* by Sam Veffer. *Missiles Masks And Miracles* was first published in 1993 by the Executive Learning Center, Aish HaTorah Jerusalem. A revised edition will be published in 1995 by **Leviathan Press:** *Books That Make A Difference.*

MISSILES MASKS AND MIRACLES

The Return of Nebuchadnezzar

In the seventh century BCE the Babylonians conquered the Asyrian empire in Mesopotamia. Under the regime of Nebuchadnezzar, Babylonia became the most powerful nation in the world. Nebuchadnezzar ruthlessly attacked his neighbors, annexing them to his own kingdom.

Early in the sixth century BCE Nebuchadnezzar's army invaded Israel. It met little resistance and quickly ravaged the country. The Babylonians destroyed the First Temple and defiled the pillaged holy sites. The Jews were conquered, and atrocities were committed. The population was taken captive and exiled to Babylonia, along with their treasures of gold and precious religious artifacts. The stolen wealth from his many conquered neighbors was used to support Nebuchadnezzar's army and build monuments to his own glory. It was in his capital city that Nebuchadnezzar built the legendary Hanging Garden of Babylon. In testimony to his grandeur, each brick was inscribed with Nebuchadnezzar's name. *By the rivers of Babylon, the Children of Israel sat and wept, and remembered Zion.* (Psalms 137:1)

North of the ancient city of Ur, also on the Euphrates River, lies the biblical city of Babylon. Years ago, Saddam Hussein commissioned archaeologists to restore the city and its Hanging Gardens. Each new brick that was added was inscribed with Saddam's name. This became a powerful symbol for him. Saddam Hussein believed that he was the reincarnation of the great Nebuchadnezzar, and dreamed of restoring the Babylonian empire to its former size and glory. During the course of the dig, archaeologists uncovered a plaque on the right-hand side of the ancient city gate. This plaque had been placed there by Nebuchadnezzar and proclaimed the ancient ruler's greatness. Saddam ordered stonemasons to place another plaque opposite the one he found, on the left-hand side of the gate, glorifying the greatness of Saddam Hussein. With his national symbol in place, Saddam then embarked on a campaign of terror, first in Iran, then in Kuwait. Ultimately, he dreamed of recapturing Jerusalem.

The Allies vs Saddam : Saddam vs the Jews

*B*etween the time the siren went off and the explosion, I didn't have time to put on my gas mask. Then the lights went out and I couldn't even find the mask. After the explosion a cloud of dust filled the whole apartment. I thought it was gas, and I didn't have my mask on.

I was lucky to be in the living room at the time and not in my tiny bedroom which had been made into my sealed room. The glass panes in the bedroom door had blown through the protective plastic sheet. Pieces of glass were all over the bed where I would have been lying. The whole room sort of squeezed in. It looked like a whirlwind of glass.

Before the big blast hit, I heard some explosions and thought the missile was overshooting my street. It must have been the Patriots partially hitting the Scud. A few moments later came the big explosion. It rocked the whole building. A piece of glass slashed through my sweater and cut my arm.

Outside there was a smell of sulfur and explosives in the air. The neighbors were staggering out of their homes, hysterical with shock and fear. One house looked almost blown apart, only its concrete frame was standing. Ceramic roof tiles were scattered everywhere. Windows were blown out with their frames. The concrete roof of a garage crashed into the windshield of a new Oldsmobile.

Another woman was standing beside what was left of her car trying to make a call on the mobile phone, while her daughter held up the antenna that had been ripped off.

Soon the streets were filled with neighbors, rescue workers and soldiers. The noise was terrible. There were ambulance sirens, burglar alarms that were triggered by the explosion, people crying and rescue workers shouting orders.

In the middle of the pandemonium a shopkeeper replaced the smashed windows of her clothing store with a large cardboard sign which said, "In spite of Saddam, we will be open for business as usual on Saturday night."[1]

Every time the siren went off, the phone rang. It was my mother in Washington D.C., tuned to CNN's live coverage, calling to make sure her adult children in Jerusalem were gathered in their sealed rooms and that they were wearing their gas masks. On one occasion, when the siren in Tel Aviv went off before the one in Jerusalem sounded, so did the phone.

T he siren just went off," my mother insisted, despite our denials, "and it will sound in Jerusalem any minute, too." Sure enough, it did. She told us what the American networks were broadcasting. It created the feeling that we were going through it all together.

Then, when the all-clear siren went off, she called again to see that we removed our masks and, even from such a distance, shuffled us all back to bed![2]

Operation Exodus. The Russians are Coming Home

As they came down the ramp from the plane, many kissed the ground. Sadly, the first gift they received upon their arrival was a gas mask. Many went immediately to visit friends and relatives who had already settled into their own homes. Most of them chose to live in the center of the country, some in Ramat Gan.

1. S.J. Ramat Gan.   2. S.C. Jerusalem.

We were staying in a neighborhood in southern Tel Aviv during the first missile attack, visiting with other Russian immigrants who were living in the area. Many of the people in the poorer houses of the neighborhood had not bothered to prepare a sealed room, so when the siren went off we all rushed to the nearby public bomb shelter. The shelter was huge and it was located inside a large public building made of concrete and metal.

About two hundred people gathered together to seek shelter inside the formidable building. A number of us moved to the wall on the eastern side of the shelter. If required, that side of the shelter served as a synagogue and the wall was filled with prayer books, Bibles and other Torah books. People were reciting Psalms over the sound of crying babies. And then came the explosion. Everything came crashing down around us. The shelter had taken a direct hit by a missile carrying five-hundred and fifty pounds of explosives. There was a smell of burning sulfur, and a thick cloud of dust filled the room.

Some of the people were thrown into the air. Others had thrown themselves to the ground and were screaming wildly. When the noise stopped and the dust began to clear, the people who had been frozen in shock began to get up and look around. Everyone was totally astonished to see that not one of the two hundred people were touched.

The next morning the Prime Minister visited the area with the Mayor of Tel Aviv. Mr. Shamir asked in astonishment if there really were people in the shelter at the time of the attack. Mayor Lahot answered that indeed , there were two hundred, and all were saved by a miracle.[1]

When the Israeli authorities prepared emergency medical facilities, they outfitted hospitals to absorb up to six thousand casualties in a single attack. Their estimates were based on the results of Scud attacks on Teheran during the Iran-Iraq war. Many Jews who lived in Teheran at the time managed to flee and resettle in Israel. Now, Saddam's missiles were following them to Tel Aviv.

---

1. *Mishpacha*, Special War Edition (p.31).

I'm originally from Iran where I lived under the regime of Khomeni. In fact, I'm a graduate of Scud attacks in Teheran. This particular evening, I went up to the fourth floor in order to help an invalid who lives there. I fed him, cleaned up the dishes afterwards, and as I was leaving his apartment I heard the siren and immediately after, the explosion. I don't know how, but to my surprise I found myself on the first floor between some blocks of concrete.

After the noise subsided, I peeked into my blown open apartment and discovered that my sealed room was totally destroyed. If I would have been in the sealed room at the time of the blast, I wouldn't be alive.

I said jokingly to my neighbor who also survived, and who is originally from Baghdad, that it looks like Saddam Hussein still wants to kill Iranians, no matter where they are. The destruction in the Ramat Gan neighborhood reminds me of the scenes of destruction from Teheran. There, the Scud missiles were much more deadly. Every Scud attack ended with tens of people killed and many more seriously wounded. People arrived at the hospitals with limbs torn off. Nurses and doctors suffered because of the damage they had to witness and repair.

The horror of the missiles was really what brought an end to the Iran-Iraq war that dragged on for eight years. Teheran turned into a ghost town, but Khomeni's people made a law so that any person who didn't go to work would be fired immediately, without severance pay, and would be publicly declared an enemy of the people. People were forced into the streets without gas masks. Fear was in their eyes. The government didn't worry about appropriate protective gear for the population and didn't compensate the victims for any damage. Anyone who lost his home had to take care of himself by begging for mercy. The economy was in a shambles. Children were out of school. Whole streets were wiped out.

When you compare the human and material loss, and the psychological damage that was done in Teheran to what has happened in Ramat Gan, it makes it easier to see the hand of Providence. Both in Tel Aviv and Ramat Gan, in spite of the great destruction, the injuries in human terms were miniscule.[1]

Mishpacha, Special War Edition (p.24).

Summing up the damage inflicted on his neighborhood during the first Scud attack that scored a direct hit was Zvi, a journalist.

"The sight was horrifying. 'Miracle' is too small a word to describe the fine line between the bloody massacre that might have taken place here, and the small numbers of lightly wounded that actually occurred."[1]

When asked to comment on the damage caused by the Scud missiles, Minister of Defense Moshe Arens had this to say:

"We see sights of destruction in Israel that have not been seen in Western countries since World War II."[2]

When one person manages to escape death, we say they were lucky. When a few people are involved, we are amazed how they cheated fate. When dozens and even hundreds of people walk away from the devastating horror of a missile attack, they have defied all laws of chance and probability.

We are a fairly traditional Jewish family from Baghdad. On Friday nights I light the candles and my husband says the Kiddush over the wine. Just after we finished Kiddush this particular Friday night, the siren went off. We managed to get into our sealed room along with our visiting nine-year-old granddaughter. Suddenly the door was torn from its place and flew through the air, landing on the backs of our necks like a wall shielding us. Then came the terrible blast from the shock wave and the window shattered with tremendous force. Splinters of glass were sprayed onto everything. After the noise quieted down, we were shocked by the power of the blast. Pieces of glass were stuck into the wall an inch deep. The door was filled with holes. Pictures on the walls were punctured. If the door wouldn't have uprooted itself and landed at the angle that it did on our necks, we would have been seriously injured by the hailstorm of glass. We saw the hand of G-d, he protected us, and in His mercy we were saved.[3]

When the siren sounded at about 2:00 a.m., Meir and his brothers — neighbors of mine from the building next door — came to me and asked me not to stay at home alone. I guess they fig-

1..*Hadashot*, Jan. 20, 1991   2. Jerusalem Post, Feb. 12, 1991

3. *Mishpacha,* Special War Edition.

ured an old lady like me couldn't take care of herself in the middle of the night. They asked me to return with them to their house to wait out the attack. They said they wanted me to feel more secure. I agreed. A few seconds later, just as we left my house, and just before we reached theirs, the missile fell in the alley right between my house and theirs, totally destroying both houses.[1]

The End is Just the Beginning

The streets of Tel Aviv are filled with children and adults wearing masks. This time they are not gas masks, but the traditional costumes celebrating the Jewish festival of Purim. People are walking to synagogue, carrying their gas masks in boxes slung over their shoulders. It is the morning of February 28, 1991. Inside the synagogues, the Book of Esther is read aloud. It is the story of a great turn of events for the Jewish people. The wicked viceroy of Persia, Haman, had plotted to murder all the Jews in the kingdom. Through a sequence of inexplicable and miraculous events, the tables were turned, and through the efforts of the Jewish leaders Mordecai and Esther, Haman was hung on the very day that he chose to kill the Jews. For 2,500 years Purim has been a day to celebrate the triumph of good over evil.

When I returned from synagogue that morning, my children greeted me with singing and laughing. While we had been reading about the destruction of Haman, George Bush had announced that the Allied forces called a cease fire. My six-year old asked if they would write a book about Saddam Hussein that would be read in synagogue next year! I smiled. In her own way, she could sense the cycle of history repeating itself.

Later that morning, at 10:00 a.m., Brigadier General Nachman Shai announced that everyone could remove the plastic sheeting from their windows and put away their gas masks. The threat of Scud missiles was over. We could start getting back to normal.

I rushed to the bedroom and ripped the brown plastic tape off the door and window frames. In my mind's eye, I again saw my family huddled together in our sealed room only a few days before. A thought

---

1. *Yediot Achronot*, Jan. 20, 1991

occurred that gave me hope for the future. My daughter's comment about Saddam recalled our people's history of 2,000 years of exile. We Jews have been scattered to the four corners of the earth. Wherever we went, we were plagued by persecution, pogroms, and the Holocaust. Ironically, while all the enemies of the Jewish people eventually disappeared, the Jews themselves survived.

I recalled the "all clear" being sounded for the last time. The announcement was made in foreign languages for those who had not yet learned Hebrew. For five minutes, the room was filled with a stream of voices, French, English, Russian, Rumanian and Ethiopian. These were just some of the languages Jews had learned in their long exile. That's when I realized I was witnessing the biggest miracle of all. The Jewish people were finally coming home.[1]

---

1. S.C. Tel Aviv.

ABOUT THE AUTHOR

Shimon Apisdorf is a rabbi who studied at the University of Cincinnati, Telshe Yeshiva of Cleveland and Yeshivat Aish HaTorah in Jerusalem. He is the founder of Leviathan Press: Books That Make A Difference, enjoys taking long walks with his wife, building snowmen with his children and cheering for the Browns with his father. His first book, *The Rosh Hashanah Yom Kippur Survival Kit* was the recipient of a Benjamin Franklin Award and his second book, *The Passover Survival Kit* has won international acclaim. These books speak clearly to a generation grappling with issues of spirituality, identity and personal growth. For speaking engagements call, 1-800-538-4284.